Celest and the Crystal Bracelet

Written by
Jill Atkins

Illustrated by
Richard Watson

It was Celest's first day at the **School for Snoops**.

All the pupils met in the classroom. Celest sat with her friends. Her best friend, Chris, sat next to her.

In marched Mrs Chevron.

"It's good to see you all," she called. "We must begin the first lesson at once."

Celest and Chris followed Mrs Chevron into a different room.

It was full of telescopes, magnifying glasses, magnets and sticks of celery.

Mrs Chevron pointed at the equipment. "These are for looking for clues," she said.

"What's the celery for?" asked Celest.

Mrs Chevron grinned. "It's a secret weapon," she said. "You may find it very handy."

Then the phone rang. It made Celest jump.

Mrs Chevron picked up the phone.

"When?" she asked. "Who? Where?"

She waited for the reply, then put the phone down.

"Right!" she said, as she turned to face the pupils. "You have a test. Charlotta Grey has lost her crystal bracelet. Celest and Chris, you must go at once and try to find it."

Celest shivered with excitement. She picked up a telescope and ran to the window.

"I can see Charlotta Grey's place," she called. "Let's go!"

Chris grabbed a magnifying glass.

"Don't forget the celery!" called Mrs Chevron. "You might need it."

Armed with their celery, Celest and Chris ran along the road.

They stopped at Charlotta Grey's place.

"Let's creep round the back," whispered Celest.

They reached the back garden.

"Let's look for clues," whispered Chris.

But they found no footprints on the ground.
They saw no fingerprints on the window sill.

There were no cracks in the window.
There was no one hidden in the bushes.

Celest felt disappointed.

"We will fail the first test if we don't find the bracelet," she said.

Then there was a sudden sound behind them. Celest jumped up and held out her celery.

"It's just a ginger cat!" said Chris.

But Celest had spotted something.

"Look!" she cried. "The cat has a new necklace."

Chris laughed. "It's made of bright gem stones!" he said.

"It's the missing crystal bracelet!" shouted Celest.

They unhooked the bracelet from around the cat's neck. Then they tapped on a window.

Charlotta Grey opened the window.

"Oh thank you!" she exclaimed. "Now I'm so happy! Please, come in and have some tea."

They had crumpets and cucumber and … celery!

"So celery isn't a secret weapon after all!" laughed Celest, as she crunched away.